WOODLAND WILDLIFE

Red Foxes

by G. G. Lake

Raintree is an imprint of Capstone Global Library Limited, a company incorporated in England and Wales having its registered office at 264 Banbury Road, Oxford, OX2 7DY – Registered company number: 6695582

www.raintree.co.uk
myorders@raintree.co.uk

Edited by Gena Chester
Designed by Juliette Peters
Picture research by Wanda Winch
Production by Steve Walker
Printed and bound in China

ISBN 978 1 4747 2183 7 (hardback)
20 19 18 17 16
10 9 8 7 6 5 4 3 2 1

ISBN 978 1 4747 2186 8 (paperback)
21 20 19 18 17
10 9 8 7 6 5 4 3 2 1

British Library Cataloguing in Publication Data
A full catalogue record for this book is available from the British Library.

Acknowledgements
Dreamstime: Menno67, 17; Shutterstock: alicedaniel, illustrated forest items, Anna Subbotina, 22-23, AR Pictures,tree bark design, Bildagentur Zoonar GmbH, 13, Daniel Hebert, 15, Darlene Hewson, 9, elina, 24, Holly Kuchera, 19, Andrew Astbury, 5, Mark Bridger, cover, Menno Schaefer, 11 (top), 21, mythja, 1, Pim Leijen, 7, Stawek, 11 (map), Sunny Forest, 3

Contents

Red foxes

The stars twinkle high above the trees.

A red fox roams the woods.

Its pointed nose sniffs the air for food.

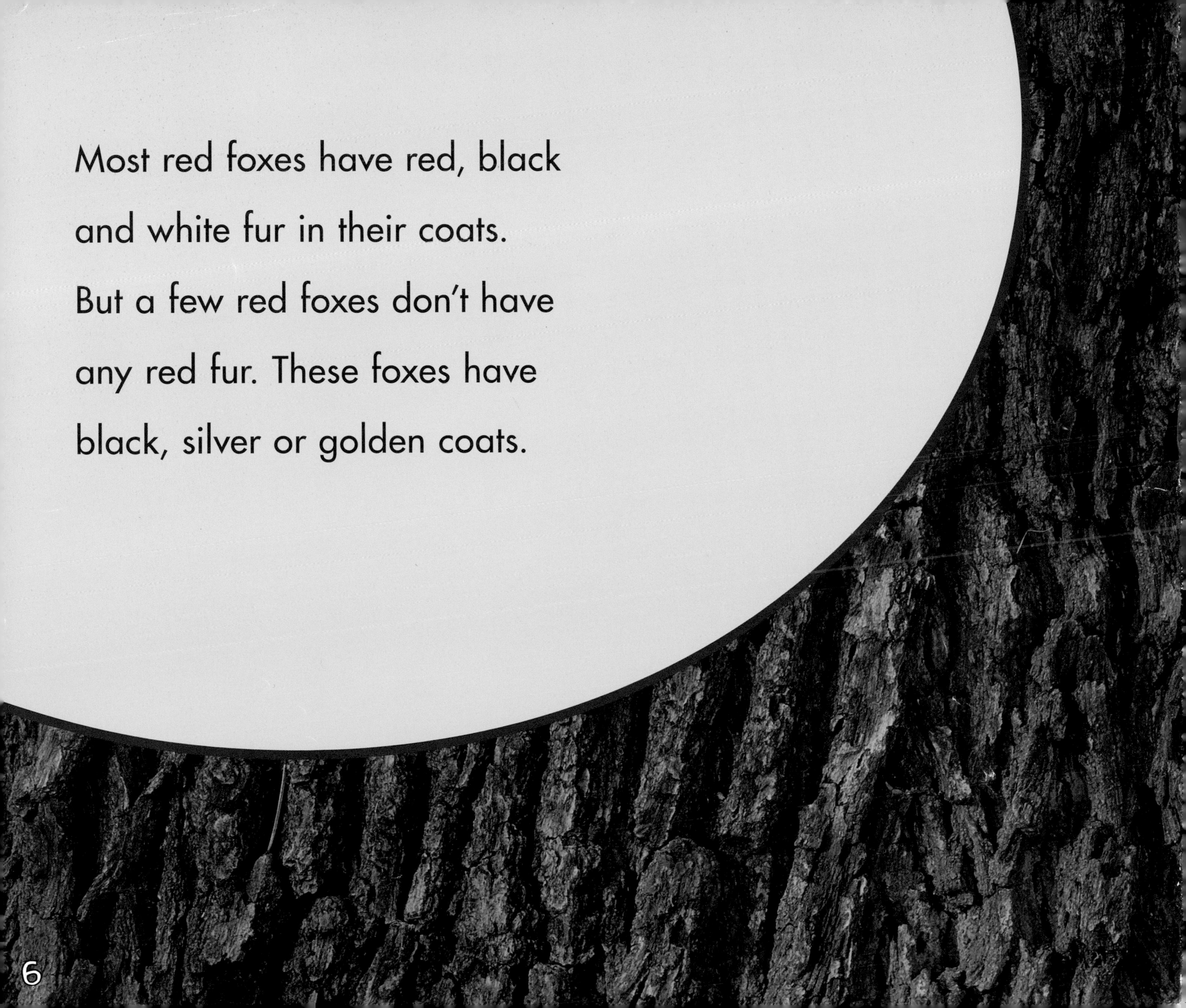

Most red foxes have red, black and white fur in their coats. But a few red foxes don't have any red fur. These foxes have black, silver or golden coats.

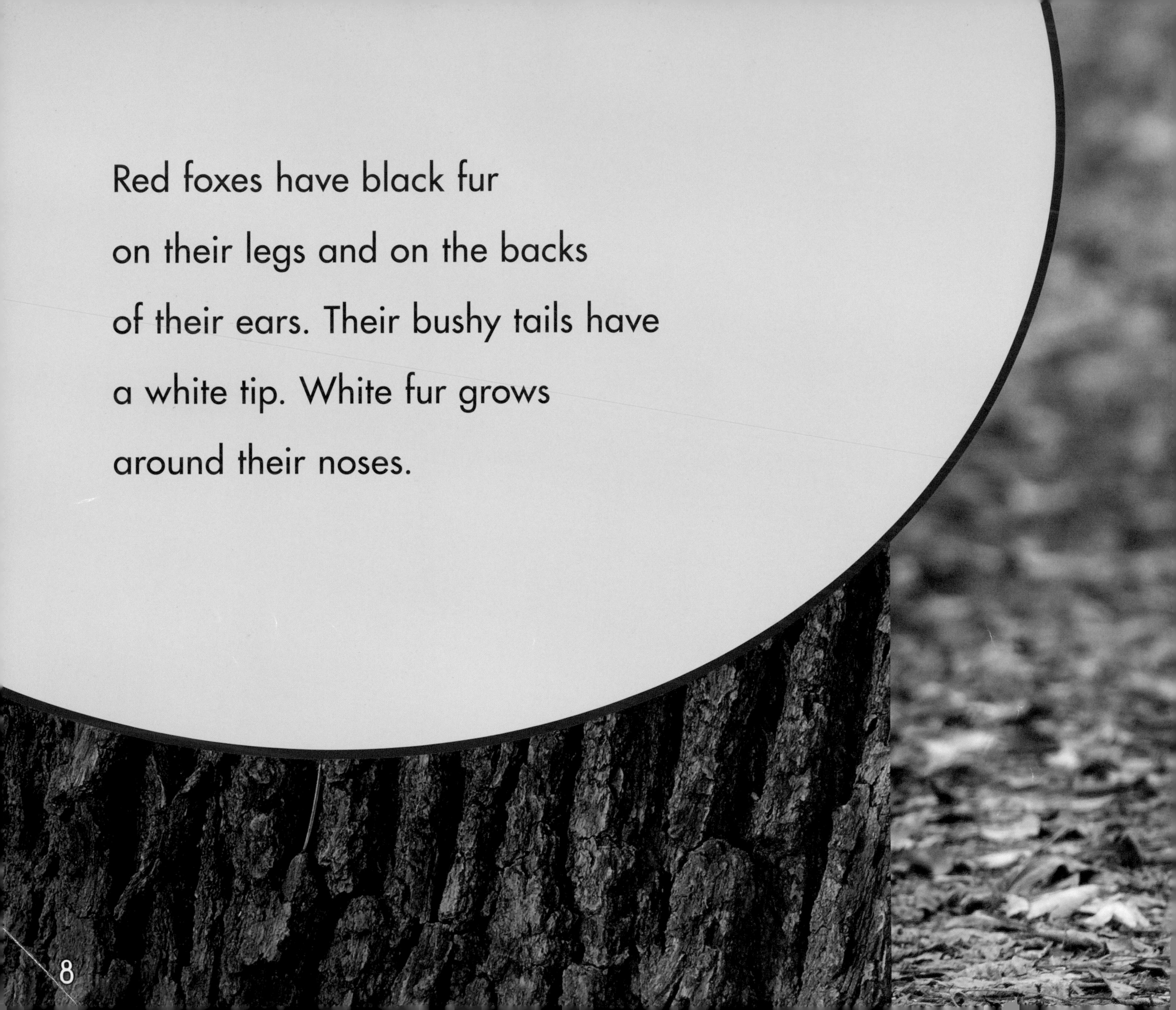

Red foxes have black fur
on their legs and on the backs
of their ears. Their bushy tails have
a white tip. White fur grows
around their noses.

Homes

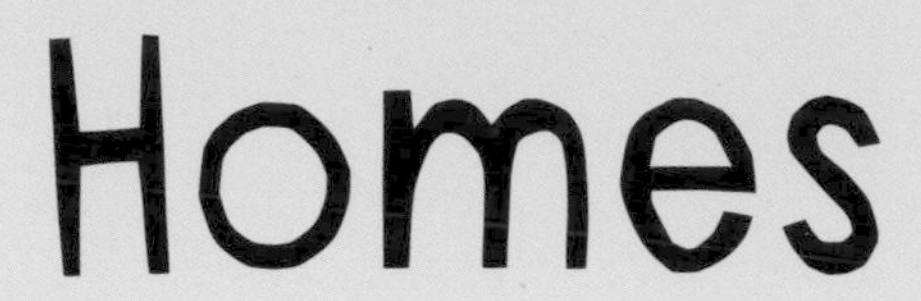

Foxes live in many places. They may live in deserts or near mountains. But they usually live in woods and near meadows.

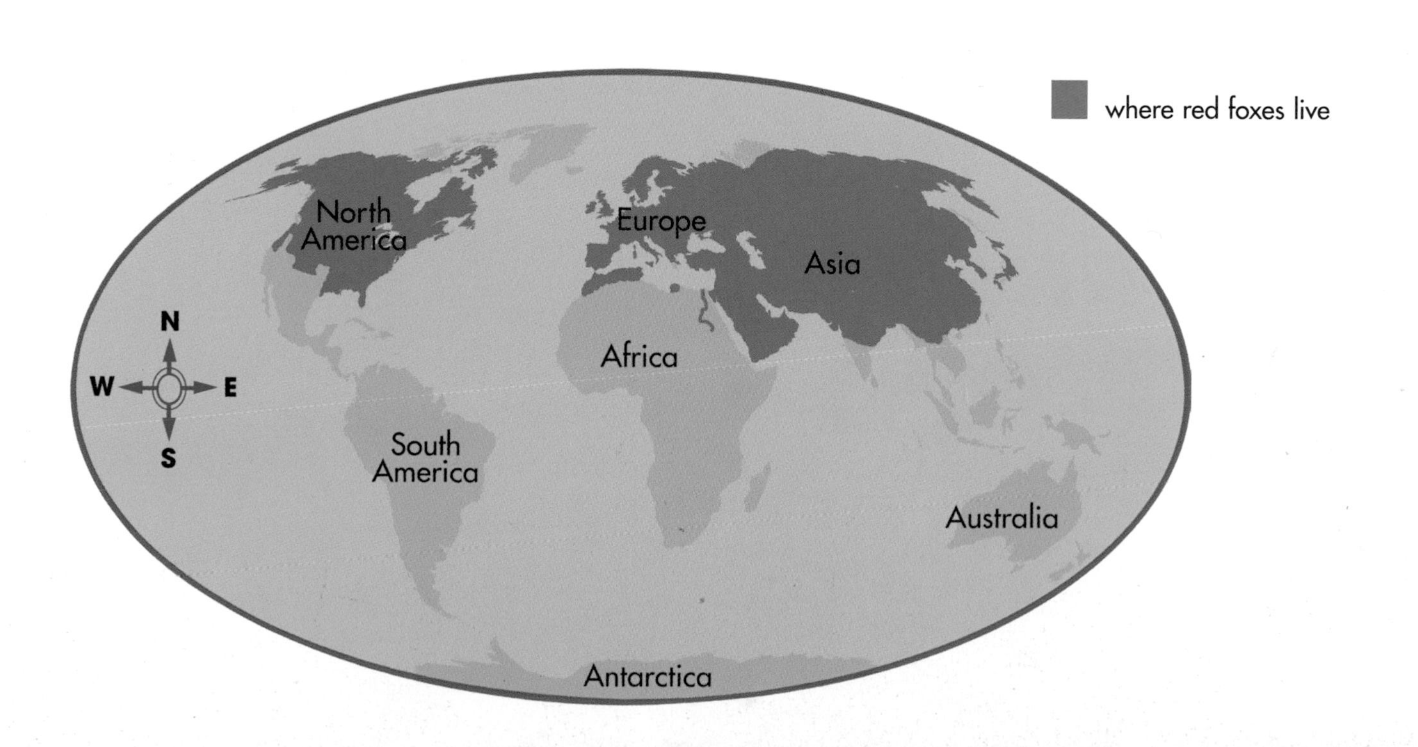
where red foxes live
North America
Europe
Asia
Africa
South America
Australia
Antarctica
N
W
E
S

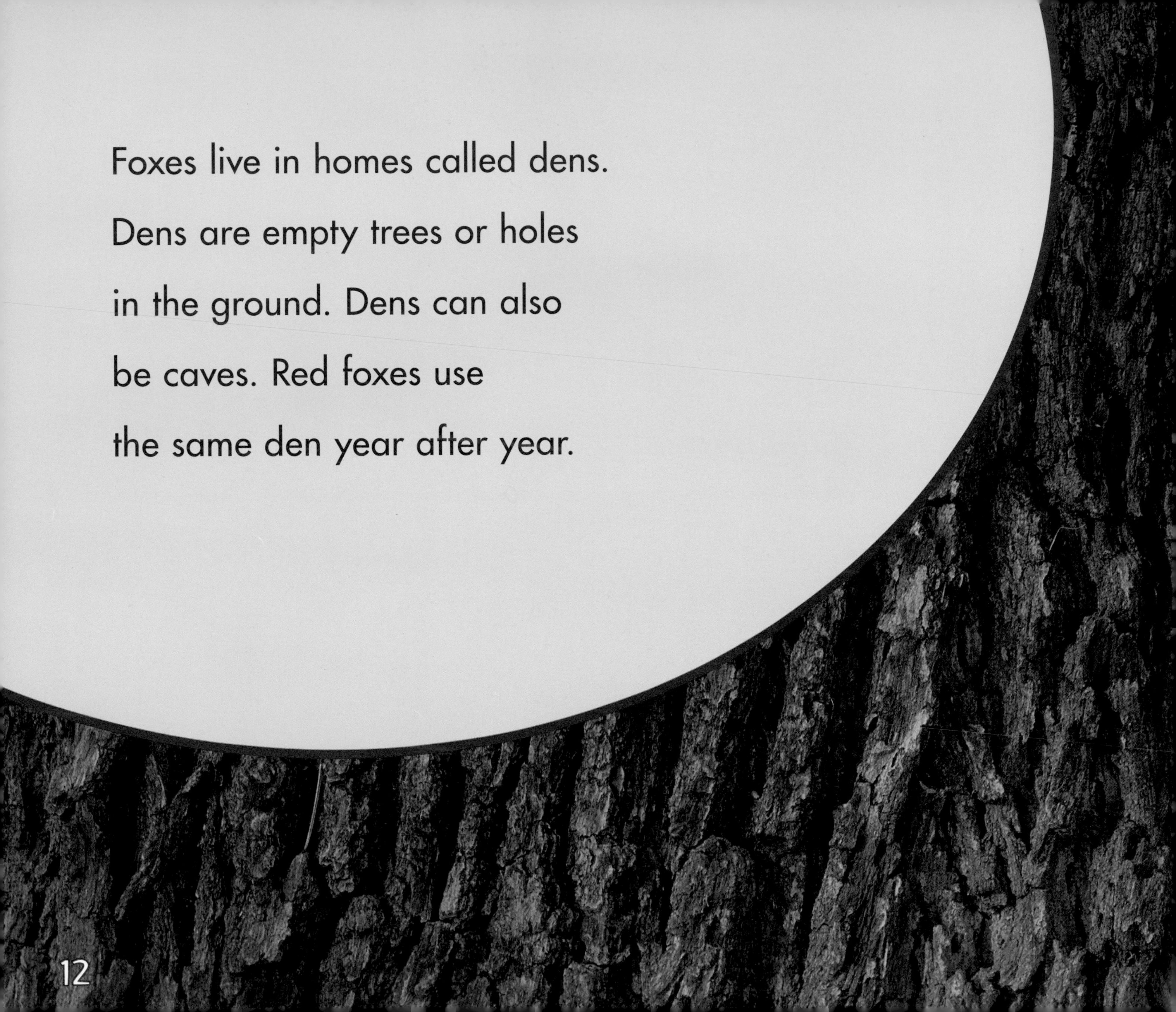

Foxes live in homes called dens.
Dens are empty trees or holes
in the ground. Dens can also
be caves. Red foxes use
the same den year after year.

Hunting

Red foxes hunt alone at night. They usually eat rodents and other small animals. Foxes use their sense of smell to find rodent dens.

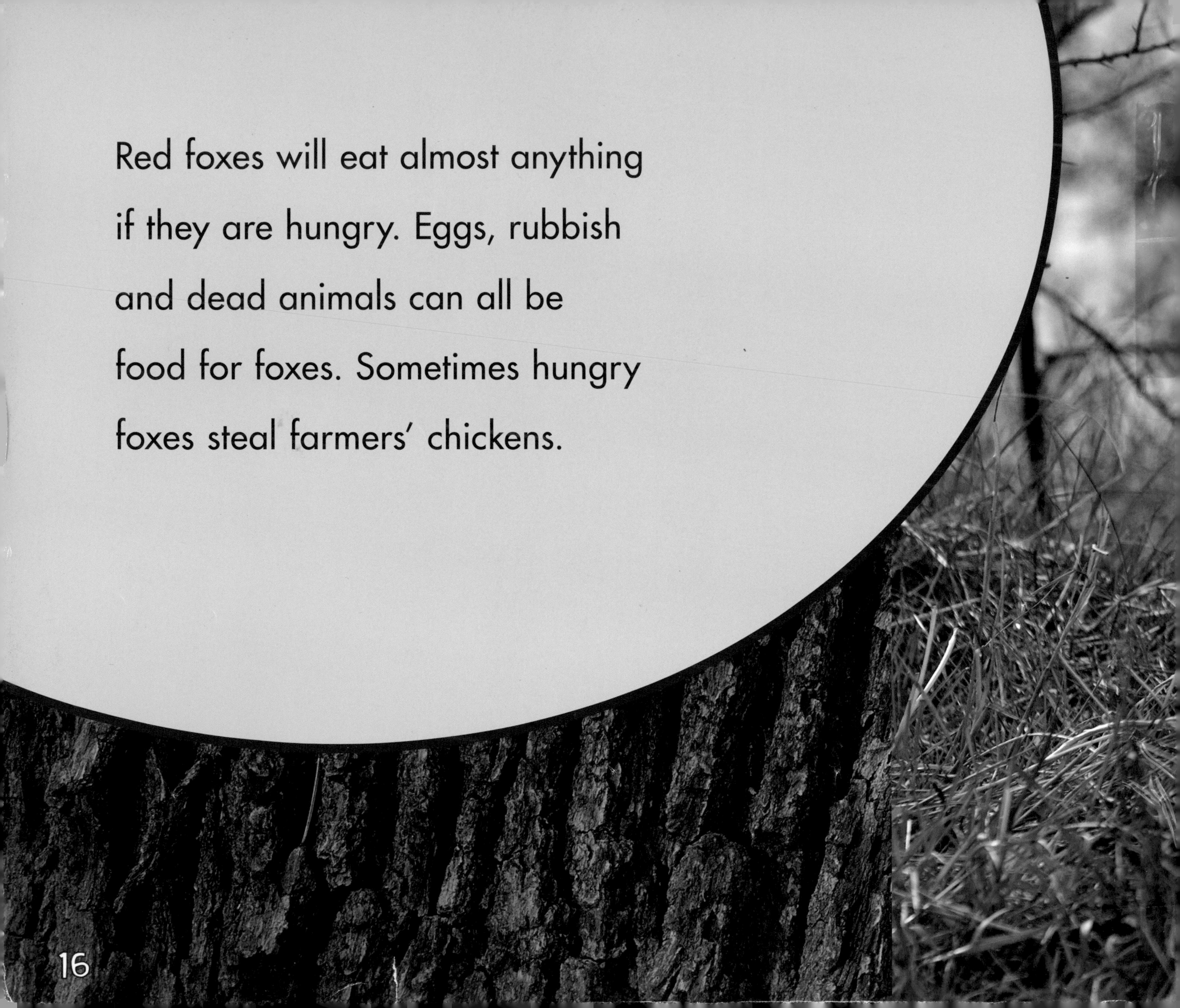

Red foxes will eat almost anything if they are hungry. Eggs, rubbish and dead animals can all be food for foxes. Sometimes hungry foxes steal farmers' chickens.

Fox cubs

Female foxes can have up to ten babies at a time. Baby foxes are called cubs. The cubs are born grey. Their fur changes colour after a month.

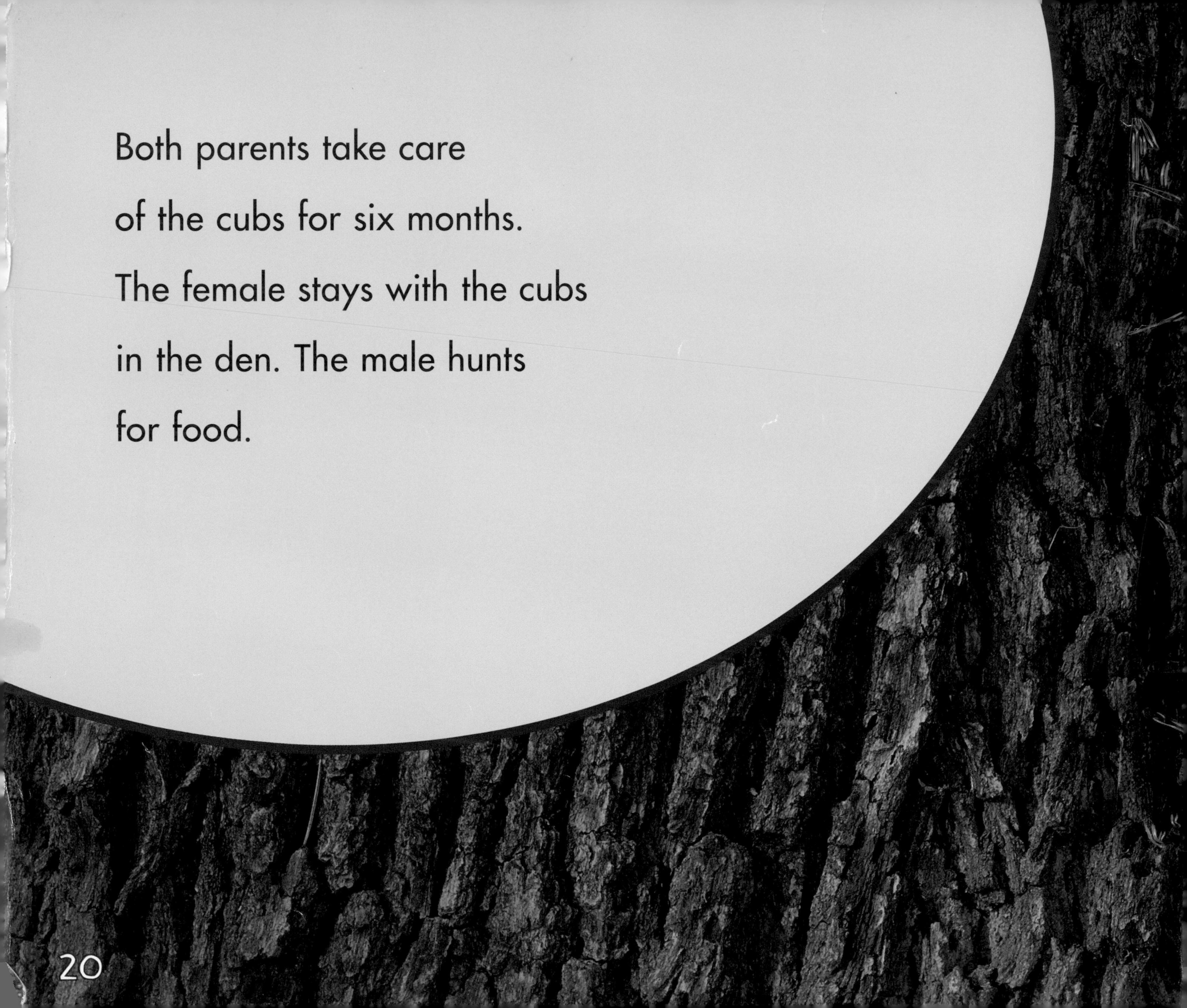

Both parents take care
of the cubs for six months.
The female stays with the cubs
in the den. The male hunts
for food.

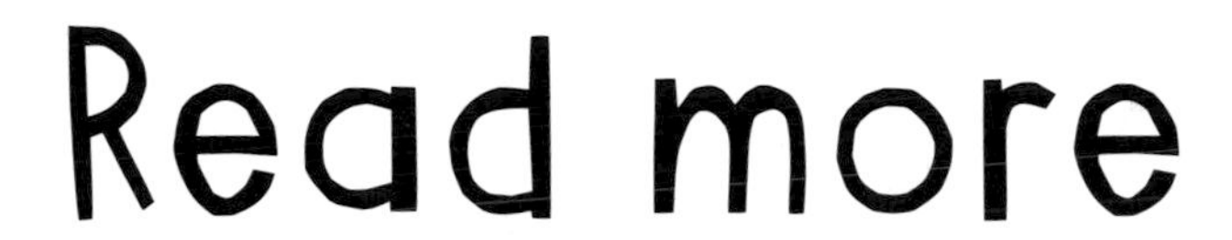

Read more

A Nature Walk in the Woods (Nature Walks), Louise and Richard Spilsbury (Raintree, 2015)

Fox (City Safari), Isabel Thomas (Raintree, 2014)

Red Foxes (Night Safari), Rebecca Rissman (Raintree, 2015)

Websites

www.bbc.co.uk/nature/life/Red_Fox
Discover more about the red fox.

www.wildlifetrusts.org/species/red-fox
Find out more about red foxes, including when and where to spot them!

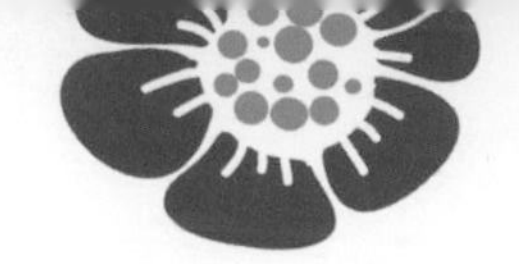

Comprehension questions

1. Why do you think farmers might not like red foxes?
2. What different colours of fur can a red fox have?
3. What is a den?

Index